The Mystery of Things

CLIVE WILMER was born in Harrogate in 1945, grew up in London and was educated at King's College, Cambridge. He now teaches English at Cambridge, where he is a Fellow of Sidney Sussex College, a Bye-Fellow of Fitzwilliam College, and an Honorary Fellow of Anglia Ruskin University. *The Mystery of Things* is his fifth Carcanet collection, the last being *Selected Poems* (1995). He has also published two volumes with the Worple Press, *The Falls* (2000) and *Stigmata* (2005). Clive Wilmer is an authority on John Ruskin and his contemporaries, and has edited selections of Ruskin, William Morris and, for Carcanet/Fyfield books, Dante Gabriel Rossetti. He is a Director of the Guild of St George (founded by Ruskin) and Principal Tutor on 'The Ruskin Journey'. He has edited the essays of Thom Gunn and, in two Carcanet volumes, Donald Davie. With George Gömöri, he has translated widely from modern Hungarian poetry, notably the work of Miklós Radnóti and György Petri; in 2005 he was awarded the annual Pro Cultura Hungarica medal for translation by the Hungarian Ministry of Culture. An occasional broadcaster, he fronted BBC Radio 3's *Poet of the Month* programmes and his interviews are published by Carcanet as *Poets Talking*.

Also by Clive Wilmer from Carcanet

CLIVE WILMER

The Mystery of Things

CARCANET

First published in Great Britain in 2006 by
Carcanet Press Limited
Alliance House
Cross Street
Manchester M2 7AQ

A CIP catalogue record for this book is available from the British Library

ISBN 1 85754 824 8
978 1 85754 824 2

The publisher acknowledges financial assistance from Arts Council England

Typeset by XL Publishing Services, Tiverton
Printed and bound in England by SRP Ltd, Exeter

To the Memory of Masters and Friends

Donald Davie
Charles Cuddon
Michael Bulkley
Tony Tanner
Edgar Bowers
Thom Gunn

ché 'n la mente m'è fitta, e or mi accora,
la cara e buona imagine paterna
di voi quando nel mondo ad ora ad ora

m'insegnavate come l'uom s'etterna;
e quant'io l'abbia in grado mentr'io vivo
convien che nella mia lingua si scerna.

INFERNO XV

…for in my memory is fixed – now it pierces my heart – the dear, kind, paternal image I have of you, when in the world, hour by hour, you taught me how man makes himself eternal; and it is right and proper that, as long as I live, my gratitude for that is shown in my language.

Acknowledgements

Thanks are due to the editors and publishers of the various publications in which these poems have appeared. 'Stigmata' was first published in *The London Magazine*. It subsequently appeared as a pamphlet: *Stigmata* (Worple Press, 2005). 'Visitation', 'The Holy of Holies', 'A Vision', 'W.S. Graham Reading' and 'The Falls' were included in *The Falls* (Worple Press, 2000). 'At Great Coxwell' was published in *The Way You Say the World: A Celebration for Anne Stevenson* (Shoestring Press, 2003) and in the Worple Press Catalogue, 2002–2003. 'Bottom's Dream' was commissioned for publication in *Around the Globe*, the magazine of Shakespeare's Globe Theatre. Other poems first appeared in the following periodicals: *Agenda*, the *London Review of Books*, *Poetry Review*, *PN Review*, *The London Magazine* and *The Reader*.

Notes to 'Stigmata'

'The Visit to La Verna' (p. 46) refers to the Franciscan monastery on Mount La Verna, Tuscany, which includes the place where, a year before his death, St Francis of Assisi received the wounds of Christ.

The italicised line in 'A Quotation' (p. 47) is from my poem 'Two Journals' published in both *Of Earthly Paradise* (Carcanet Press, 1993) and *Selected Poems* (Carcanet Press, 1995).

Contents

I

II

I

[We'll] take upon's the mystery of things
As if we were God's spies

KING LEAR

Bottom's Dream

It shall be called 'Bottom's Dream', because it hath no bottom...

I was a weaver, and I wove
The moody fabric of my dream.
By day I laboured at the loom
And glimpsed the image of a love
   I now know bottomless.

We were young men. We played our parts.
We schooled ourselves in the quiet wood.
By night the moon, which draws the flood,
Tugged at the rhythms of our hearts.
   And they were bottomless.

I loved a girl who was a boy;
I took my stand and beat my breast.
Yet what was I but fool and beast,
Who did not so much speak as bray,
   In bombast bottomless?

I trusted I had mastery,
Until one night, being left alone,
I snorted at the wandering moon
In terror of the mystery,
   Which seemed quite bottomless,

And out of that *she* spoke, who had
No voice, although she stirred my sense,
Who touched me, though she had no hands,
And led me where you cannot lead,
   Since it is bottomless.

I tried to speak: again I brayed.
I pinched and scratched my face: coarse hairs
Were crisping over cheeks and ears.
And when she drew me in, she made
   The whole world bottomless.

Nothing possessed me. So she said
Do not desire to leave this wood.
Among the mossy clefts I hid
With petals where she pressed my head,
       Desire being bottomless.

A most rare vision, such a thing
As who should say what such things be:
My terror turned to ecstasy,
The one much like the other, being
       Both of them bottomless.

And then the change. The sun came up
Brash as a brassy hunting-horn.
I woke and, yes, I was a man.
Was I myself though? Self, like sleep,
       May well be bottomless.

New moon tonight. Another dream
To act. They laugh at our dismay.
Oh but it's nothing. Only play.
Except we just don't feel the same,
       For play is bottomless.

And so the story ends. My eyes
Are sore with weeping, but I laugh
(I who was seen to take my life),
For, having been an ass, I'm wise
       And bottomless. Bottomless.

Dog Rose in June

Pink petals flare in the hedge:
Rosa canina, rose of the dog days.
Gently I splay the petals, bend and sniff.
The whole flower gives off sweetness,
Pungency deeper in.
Such heat this evening, come away from the path.

Who are you that have stepped into the light
    so unforeseeably
    that 'goddess' seems the word?
    how else to name

that beauty more than beauty, inwardness
    so perfectly made flesh
    we are abased by it
    and almost fear

there will be no way back – though to come back,
    the vision thus relinquished,
    is what we least desire?
    I most desire

you here and now, although, till here and now,
    I could not yet have wanted
    what still remained unknown –
    except we're told,

there'd be no dream of earthly paradise
    without the fallen earth.
    Your body is a thing
    as the earth is

but with the fragrance of another world...
    O gentle girl, who tremble
    when you are touched, whom I
    tremble to touch,

you rend the dark like lightning, leaving day
    solemn with ravage, yet
    bright with the evidence
    of visitation.

Wonderwoman

I lay where I had fallen
Naked on the floor, alone, unable to stand –
And waited for the ambulance. This was to mean
Complete surrender to another's will.

She appeared at the window-sill
And dropped in over the top half of the sash:
Pale blonde hair drawn back, sand-white at the brow,
And eyes like summer sky
And a gold tan running deep into her cleavage
And a perfume something to do with flowers and the salt smell of the sea.

I felt the discourtesy
Of not rising to greet her. Nonetheless,
She gathered me up, bore me almost, carried me away.
What could I do?
I was like Odysseus in Circe's arms, enthralled,
But in my helplessness
Not quite believing I was not a pig,
And yet knowing myself, inside myself,
Moved to my best of inwardness.

You at your book. Me unable to read,
supposing that I get between your words
as, fingers twined in your hair or stroking your neck,
    you nonetheless read on.

Since you will not answer letters or calls
or nod to me in the street, I will write to the moon
or else to the image I have of you in my mind,
    which is all responsiveness.

Either way, fearing that I might touch,
you fend me off by scowling into a book;
but I'm there among the words, wanting to be,
    like them, read into you.

The Ruin

Cattle browse in the meadow the sprung arch,
shot of its tracery, frames

Form looking out of ruin, a different view
shaped by the form's persistence
                           Miracle,
no other word for it, the enduring face
of Andrei Rublyov's *Saviour*, gazing out
from what, after several centuries as a doorstep,
the context gone, is plainly still a board:
not Christ the judge, this one – a hurt survivor
with knowledge it is hard to look away from
of what is suffered here
                       And come again
as Radnóti's last poems from the dark
and warmth of a mass grave, which they had shared
with swathes of greatcoat and corrupting flesh,
till brought to light
                   So the old bagwoman,
raddled, incontinent, hoists her reeking skirts
and, her lips pursed for crooning, rasps aloud:
Paradise, boys, come on, you can have it now.

then broke in and found nothing.

She took me by the hand. A desolate place,
a place of stones, being unmade and made:
dark gashes in the earth with, all about,
stagnant pools, so churned up the terrain;
and standing alone, a stark new office block,
half-built and bare, its concrete white in the moon.

From destruction we may draw consolation:
that there's no escape from fate,
not for great works or even holy places.
Nevertheless, that so ravishing a building,
its materials alone – marble and cedarwood –
so sumptuous, the stone so smoothly cut
so closely joined

       Think of that
and, thinking of the place, how deep inside, there
in the Holy of Holies,
you can lose what you are,
desire to, fear to

       As I Flavius,
a soldier of fortune, not myself a Roman,
in this epoch since the fall,
trafficked with a lithe avatar of the goddess
Astarte, Aphrodite, whatever name,
in the region of King's Cross.
She it was
who led me through that place to the tall block
as yet unfinished, so that it seemed a ruin

the sanctum, the broken chancel, the lopped shaft
holier than it would have been
intact

before it, bare and empty, a white lodge,
a simple cube of space, and we went in.
One window, the moon seen through it, and the night
unseasonably warm, she threw her dress aside,
breasts and shoulders silvered by the moonlight:
she was so beautiful I could have
gone down on my knees but, as we stood there,
I ran my fingertips along her mouth, caressed
her nipples, the dome of her belly, the dark fuzz:
I thought and measured, seeking
the precise gentleness to weigh the value.

These two together.

                    Flavius
saw the Temple burn in Jerusalem,
saw it fall, with ravines for its foundations,
the superstructure not unworthy of them,
their depth, their great magnificence, their strength.
Nevertheless it fell,
the Temple of Solomon and the house of wisdom
waxed marble and scented cedarwood
fell
at the touch of flame.

The torches carved a space out of the darkness,
a recess of twenty cubits, until then
screened by a veil and unapproachable,
inviolable, invisible to all.
In it stood nothing whatever, it was called
the Holy of Holies

          lose what you are
             fear   desire

dark
        made darker still by the white ray:
she turned away from me, as if to bow
to the moon's face, but leaned on the rough sill,
so that her breasts hung softly in my hands

then the flames flared and leapt,
I pushed lightly and the entrance gave

signifying
  a lot of fuss about fucking
or even about that primal quantity
known in those days as *naught*, as naughty,
as NO THING:
    calling to mind
Courbet's *L'Origine de l'univers.*

For nothing this wide universe I call
– know what I mean? –
in it thou art my all

and all for nothing.
For nothing doing. Since nothing
shall come of nothing.
            Yea,
do on then this nought
else that thou do it for God's love and
nothing have these nothings if this be nothing
that is not there;
        and the Nothing that is
our inner man clepeth All.

Recorded Message

Here for your pleasure –
no rush –
day by day:

Dawn
Summer
Celeste

Amber
Dolores
Caprice

and Crystal
or, sometimes,
Precious.

'In a doorway, I swear.
　　　　　　There were these two –
I was late cycling home
　　　　　a gorgeous night
midsummer and people
　　　　　　out partying still.
I freewheeled past this shop
　　　　　　they were necking there
but she had her breasts out
　　　　　　one hand on his fly.
The bike sailed breezily on –
　　　　　　I did a sort of
drawn-out double-take,
　　　　　　turned back up the hill
and there she was
　　　　　on her knees now
blowing his horn.
　　　　　　Imagine
how I felt:
　　　　　like some Sicilian peasant
hailed one day
　　　　　by an angel on the dung heap –
or this girl walking ahead
　　　　　in a blue scarf
turns to accost him, he stares
　　　　　and it's the Virgin.
They're funny, Catholics: so
　　　　　literal sometimes
about the things of the spirit,
　　　　　even fleshly.'

The Ladder

...this any *place where God lets down the ladder*
John Ruskin

'Don't let go yet. What was it made you cry
Just then? Keep holding on to me. You cried
Like a new baby launched upon the world,
A singer at her pitch of ecstasy,
A trapped animal howling against pain.'

I cried?
       'As if from a shut room inside.
Not like your own: like someone else's cry
Sounding within you.'
              If it was me that cried,
Or if through me the two of us, it was
That as we grappled here we seemed to touch
Some nerve of inwardness. Let me turn preacher.
I have, in former discourse, been inclined
To speak of love as though it were a thing
Outward and visible: the which thing is
In truth a fallacy. Consider Jacob,
Who wrestled with an angel and prevailed.
Where was that angel? Or those other ones
He witnessed in a nameless desert place
Somewhere between Beersheba and Haran?
The scriptures use the figure of a ladder
Propped between land and sky to body forth
The dream he had, head pillowed on a stone,
Of angel hosts ascending and descending.
But now, from the new exegetes, we learn
Of a stark outcrop glacially planed,
A table-land, with terracing for stairs;
Or – since it was, he said, the House of God –
Of a stepped temple, a symbolic mount
Like a vast altar, from whose surface priests,
With cries to distant gods, offered up smoke,
Throwing it forth, as charred bones fell away,
A frail and ghostly bridge from earth to heaven.

'We have travelled a long way
From the dark chamber of your inwardness.
What could have caused that resonance today?'

I don't know. It was nothing. I can't say.

Bethel

When Jacob in the desert stopped
   For nightfall and the climbing stars,
He slept, a stone his pillow,
    Among volcanic scars.

He saw the angels of the Lord
   Ascending and descending there
In glory, with the Lord himself
    Above the topmost stair.

At break of day he set the stone
   An upright pillar on the ground.
It made the sky a heavenly roof
    And earth's foundation sound.

The Architect at his Mountain Villa

All I can do is take you to the edge
    And throw a belvedere
Out on the void, fenced in with cabled steel,
So there is nothing which you need to fear –
      As fear you will,
Like somebody marooned on a rock ledge.

This is what builders do: compose a space
    For you to live inside
And be in body. They can give no more
Than wood or concrete, stone or brick provide.
      All else they ignore,
Except to make a view out of a place.

What if the view were merely space? What if
    Odd atmospheric freaks –
Stray clouds, perhaps a viscous film of mist –
Were all that filled it? Floating, the snow peaks
      Barely exist –
Far less than we do, grounded in this cliff.

For my Daughter's Wedding

To Tamsin and Chris, with love

A photograph. It is a woodland place
In late spring and a girl of two or three
Looks at the camera with an earnest face
That might have just been smiling. Could that be
Fear in those soft eyes? No, it is rather trust,
Though trust derives from some first sense of fear.
But still, the woods are tranquil and buds thrust
Expansively into the genial air.

The child is now a woman who today
Turns the same earnest look toward her love,
Then laughs, her head thrown back, in her dear way.
Such fun. Such seriousness. You know them, Chris:
They make rough places kindly and they save
Our world from what might be sheer wilderness.

There are star-crystals shining white on the blank earth.
It is a visitation from on high,
Where there is nothing but exploding worlds
And radiant fragments of infinity.

Plenty

Apples,
    as if they were blossoms,
      left to drop.

Chutney

For Lyubomir Nikolov

Apples: they clogged the brook,
and the turf under the boughs
was a cobbled yard to our feet:
    do you remember?

How returning at dusk we rescued
four plastic-bagsful of them –
so ripe they were, and bruised,
    and near to rotting.

We cooked them in vinegar
with onions, garlic, sultanas,
soft brown sugar, ground ginger,
    salt and black pepper.

Jar after jar for gifts.
Yet I'm eating it still, and still
I've a store, which stores in itself
    that fruitful September –

you remember it, Lyubomir,
    I know you remember.

The Apple Trees

For Lyubomir Nikolov, again

But the trees, Lyubomir, remember the trees!
Five or six of them, each a distinct variety
Of apple – yellow or red, russet or buff-green –
With a footbridge over the brook
And a path winding among them through high grass.

One I can still see.
In the mind's eye, as then through the body's too,
I feel the gravid pull
Of the fruit bunched red among green, red as the autumn sun,
Bending the boughs.

Well, now they are gone.
Churning up rights of way,
Bulldozers plough the earth for the new block.
New rights, of course, will succeed the old, but for what?
There is always something more important than trees.

What is anger, my friend, but a form of memory?
I will not let go.
To do so, I know (so they tell me), is good for the soul.
I cannot think of that. I prefer the pain of knowing the trees lost
To losing the trees.

At Great Coxwell

Great Coxwell tithe barn (William Morris said)
'As noble as a great cathedral' – and
On the same mighty scale.
                              Arriving there
One incandescent afternoon, we saw
In the arrow-slit just over the main portal
A carrion crow alighting. It then flew
A dipping flight the length of the dark hall
To pass, without a feint at hesitation,
Out through the other slit at the far end,
The white glare momentarily gone black:

Like Bede's sparrow, with a grimmer touch.

Behold, the Fowls of the Air

For Ingrid Soren, Buddhist & Christian

1

The world is sunk in darkness.
The great light is seen by few of us.
Few birds escape the net;
Few souls attain the freedom beyond night.

2

The city judged, the red kite and the bittern
Lay claim to it, the screech-owl and the raven
Haunt the streets, the tumbled stones of chaos
Mark out the borders of its emptiness.

3

The stork on the chimney-stack knows when to leave;
Likewise, the crane, the swallow and the dove
Watch for their time. We, though, shade our eyes;
When judgement falls, it falls to our surprise.

4

Those who, young, were inwardly at war
Missed the real treasure that eludes desire.
In age, they are like the heron – lank, unfed –
By a pool empty of fish. They look sad.

5

Consider the birds of the air:
They neither reap nor sow nor store,
And yet your Father feeds them day by day.
You are, surely, more than they.

6

Even the sparrow has found a home,
And the nesting swallow room
Just near the altar of my God and King,
Where she may raise her young.

7

Is it by your wisdom and at your word
That the hawk flies, that she spreads her wings southward?
Did you bid the eagle tower? And can you brag
She builds her rough nest on the topmost crag?

8

Flight is the miracle that frees the swan
To follow the sun's path. Strong men
First conquer evil and its troops, then soar
Above the narrow space where they made war.

9

Two sparrows make a pennyworth,
Yet if just one of them should fall to earth,
Your Father knows. Your every hair
He has numbered. Do not fear.

10

The swift forsakes her home. She sweeps south,
In her wake the dark and cold, like bitter truth.
Yet she returns. Soon you will hear her wail,
As if in agony, that all is well.

Sources: *Dhammapada* 13.174; Isaiah 34.11; Job 39.26–28; *Dhammapada* 11.155;
Matthew 6.26; Psalms 84.3; Jeremiah 8.7; *Dhammapada* 13.175; Matthew 10.29–31.

I_N
PRINCIPIO
the Evangelist
rapt in contemplation of the Word,
an eagle at his ear, his slender wrist
poised over the page, the bird poised,
contemplative, predatory, for the long flight.

This is the record of John, as of the scribe
in the monks' scriptorium on the green isle
some fourteen hundred years ago, at the edge
of the known world – that world, margin to centre,
the unerring flight of a migratory bird.

Then, facing the illumination, blocks
of language, columns, they might be towers of stone
to withstand siege and temporal incursion,
born of the air, though, to be borne on air,
as on broad wings, migrating into time.

And this, the record of stone, a fine-grained
Bavarian limestone, it splits into thin slabs,
creamy and smooth – pages that, once turned,
disclose the print of fortune, left unread
a hundred-and-fifty million years and more.

It is Archaeopteryx, in the beginning,
cresting the wave of time, those first feathers
lifting it, buoying it on, until catastrophe
set it down, the molten instant set,
process, not progress, still less final form.

The gaping mouth, teeth bared, the pinions splayed,
nailed to that moment there, eternity
its inconceivable frame: this hieroglyph –
whose language, never held in mind, is silent –
launched upon prophecy, utters itself.

Word drunk they called him. Well:
I don't know about *words.*
                 He sat there turning the pages
unable to fix on a single verse
plaintive and truculent
                 quarrelling with the book,
as if to surrender to a single instance
of language
                 was to surrender.

Then: 'Read any one of them,' somebody cried:
'They're all marvellous!'
                 And we beheld a marvel:
an Archangel
                 a little damaged
igniting the dark firmament with speech.

To George Herbert

Time and again I turn to you, to poems
In which you turn from vanity to God
Time and again, as I at the line's turn
Turn through the blank space that modulates –
And so resolves – the something that you say.

The Falls

For Jim Spates

I am haunted by this memory of the falls:
The turbulent water with its bloom of froth
      Hung like a curtain, still
      Changeless and invariable;
Yet spat and spumed, dripped and cascaded, gushed –
Eased itself of the burden the great lakes
      Had urged upon it. Also,
      Viewed from the side, it stood
From the rock wall like a sheer and polished pane
At the top curved and stooping to the plunge –
      To the deep catastrophe
      That shattered it – and then
Rebounded back as star-flung spray, a deathless
Tower of it, rising, as if in worship –

*

Did Jackson Pollock
             when he painted *One*
know the Lord's beauty by it?
                      What we call
randomness –
             the white stream
lashed over brown and purple
                      sprayed and flecked –
not at all
             deep canyons of the underself
but the order in which things fall
             or what intelligence will make of them.
Draped from the rock it
                      frills but falls:
the same pattern, never
                      the same water.
You will find
             (I must tell you)
no great man
             not a man of law.

*

Further downstream we had paused at other falls:
Slight trickles, graceful cataracts, rapids, weirs,
      The still rock around which
      A rope of current tugged
And, frothing from some ledge, a watery fringe
Of tasselled elegance. Each one of them,
      For all the vehement clamour,
      Displayed rule and design;
Though they fell, they fell by the same laws,
And all such law breeds pattern. This one, however,
      Was quite another thing:
      A gulf in the earth's crust,
Chaos to us – ocean or milky way –
And order, therefore, in the larger mind.

*

the sun and the other stars
      the beating heart
           the snow-melt

driven, crying
of this steep place afraid
          the common pass

but fraying there
the vast drum of woven stuff unwinding,
          the dripped lace

no measure fine enough
eye or finger or numerate brain

immutable change
          made and remade
laws finer than any known of men

from things made
      being seen and understood
          the invisible things

each frill and fibre
          eternal power

II

To Rosamond

For nothing this wide universe I call
Save thou, my rose; in it thou art my all.

SHAKESPEARE, SONNET 109

Ghostliness

I

The host
steeped in wine
limp on my tongue,

I, for the
first time,
tasted flesh,

all day thereafter
haunted
by the ghost.

II

You beside me
sharing
the ghostly taste,

your flesh
has come so close
there is no flesh

and no spirit,
only
the twining ghosts.

Stigmata

as thou art
All my delight, so all my smart
George Herbert

I
THE VISIT TO LA VERNA

Holiness, not wholeness. If I touched
Too fiercely, just a shade so, you would bleed,
So near the skin your innermost of wounds.

*

Autumn on Mount La Verna. A gust of snow
Reminded us: Brother Donkey, the sack-cloth
Showing his ribs, at forty-three, worn through.

*

His body disciplined to stand ajar,
A threadbare sack, two sandals and a cord
Were all he had to guard it from the world.

Think of him as he must have been, the frail
And unregarded body that lay down
Nightly upon a grid in the dark cave:

A withered leaf that curls round its own form –
Though not resisting death, still on the tree,
Still of the world, simply by being there.

*

You who wake to the light of the high peaks,
Here is my darkness in this squalid cave.
But where do *you* lie down for your snow-dreams?

46

II
A Quotation

An angel here, there a tormented beast.

'The angel I can take; the beast, no.'

No choice: you must take both, or neither.

*

Neither, then. Before long, the wound heals
And leaves in a nest of scars a crescent scar,
Unseen, till again your nakedness be shown.

As It Was

A Buddha's sleek tranquillity reflects
In a glazed wood veneer. Nearby is hung
An austere body on a crucifix,
Broken with pain, though sinuously young.

On a small chair the heap of clothes you've shed
Is like a crumpled statue. You, set free
From dressed propriety, stretch out on the bed
And draw me gently to your privacy.

No soul distinct from body, love from sex:
In sensuous lines, slight wrinkles, greying hair
I read a ghostly story, and the text
Has flourishes extravagant but spare.

You look at once so strong and vulnerable,
So shaped by fortune to a discipline,
I hardly dare to touch you. Yet I feel
Scar tissue in the smoothness of your skin.

IV
THE CONVERSATION

I think of this as of a conversation
That's run through the nine months we've spent apart,
You angry, me despairing; I remember

Stray phrases from your talk, which come to me
Like those quotations out of plays or poems
That bring delight in sorrow or console.

Yours, though, torment: with bitter truth, injustice
And all that beautiful intelligence
I may no longer love. I quote you quoting

From certain of the mystics that you read –
From Meister Eckhart or the *Dhammapada*
Or visionaries in whom eternal love

Leaves open wounds. Or else I quote from Shakespeare
And you respond: 'I've been re-reading him
And thinking how he dwells, as we have noticed,

On "nothing" – "all for nothing" and all that –
So that his nothing seems the source of all things.'
More often, though: 'You have betrayed my trust.

You've such good qualities: why do you spoil them?
Please keep away. Desire for you has gone.'
But my desire persists, an unhealed lesion

Scoured with your invective, 'nothing' then
Making a nothing out of dear remembrance,
Our pool of happiness too soon dried up,

Hope hopeless, and the future without meaning –
Except, perhaps, the kind of meaning found
In Shakespeare or a silent conversation.

V

PADRE PIO

Francesco Forgione (1887–1968)

'That fucking whore-madonna...' and a fart
Of gut contempt, a man his body's functions.
They drove a spear into Francesco's heart.

Struck by his comrades. No, the Colonel said,
You could not make a man of him, the priest
No priest of him. So, without leave, he fled.

Bowels clenched, his inner force – from the assault
Contracting – shrank still further in, head split
Like continents adrift along a fault.

The Brothers took the burden on. But then
His inner world's deranged geography
Stabilised round an organising pain,

Which was the pain of Christ. Therefore not his.
He brooded as he celebrated Mass
And prayed, losing himself not to lose this.

Church hours passed. Pain, sweetened and perfumed,
Swirled through his body. Then a nameless love
Flushed at the portal of each sudden wound.

VI
SYMMETRY

'Lop-sided,' you once told me: more sensitive
On one side than the other, your right brain
More active than the left; but to attain
A self in balance was, you said, to live.

In a photograph your eyes speak, the right one
Of nurture and the force of it; the glaze
In the left, though, brings news of a cold place
It glimpsed once and will one day fix upon.

*

Monuments of the time of the Black Death
Might house two effigies: beauty above
In all its earthly splendour – like a meadow
Embroidered with the thousand flowers of May;

The other effigy, laid out beneath,
Foretells the flayed cadaver. You, my love,
Who walk with death, lie down beside his shadow,
The focused knowledge of your own decay.

He is the Life and the End to which men must come; and He is the Door...
We must enter by this Door, by breaking through nature,
and by the exercise of virtue and humility...

Johannes Tauler

In the first place, a medieval childhood:
in your father's hands
the huge key to the manor house.
A ghost passed on the far side of the wall.
Later on,
hauntings of the spirit and hormones.
Then the retreat: 'where prayer has been valid',
who is it thrusts a knife into your sternum?
An angel, you would say. If ghosts, angels:
you have need of them.

You rise from that, as on the afternoon
you drove through a thunderstorm to a sick-bed,
your mother's, as she waited for the bolt
to strike into her life,
as simultaneously, on a road awash,
it stabbed into your heart.

To live your life was to walk with death.
                                    So when –
your child dead and husband gone –
you lay down on your couch as in your grave,
you fell into another space:
a passage, a garden at the end of it, a door
opening on light, a voice within it
that spoke in concert with an unseen throng,
their scent and music promise and presage.

VIII
WALLED GARDEN

Hortus inclusus. The locked gates inspire
Trespassers: Casanova with young nuns…
The body vulnerable to its desire

Seeks out another who is vulnerable:
She, sealed in her apartness, broods within
Her body, which has served her as a wall

But, prone to ecstasy, might yet become
The means of access for a teeming world
That, touching her, would leave her chilled and numb.

It was always an illusion, that reserve.
There is no faith or hope that does not know
The odour of carnality, nor love

The neighbourhood of animals: lost sheep,
The ox and ass, the reek of stable straw,
The child at the swollen breast nodding asleep,

Who born in pain will end in pain, his bonds
Unbroken breaking him, his inwardness
Leaking into the world through his five wounds.

THE SECOND DAY

The man of sorrows sleeps, his blood congealed:
His hair is clotted with the mud that stops
All orifices, and the tomb is sealed.

It is the day of rest and there is peace.
Despair brings certainty, a sober grief
And understanding. Argument may cease.

Yesterday was the earthquake and the storm,
Crowds, horror, iron hammered into flesh,
The rending of the veil, the foretold doom.

This is the second day. The text is mute.
I am Simon Peter, Thomas Didymus,
I contemplate my guilt, I mourn, I doubt.

Oh you, my love, my fair one, dew in your hair
And roses in your cheeks, you are gone now.
Love dies with you. This is the day of care.

Tomorrow, though, will be the crux of time:
I shall be John or Mary Magdalene
And I shall stand with spices at the tomb.

X
PIERO'S *RESURRECTION* 1

For some, pagan. The dawn dimly wakes,
Like a new season, raising the dead god,
We mortals sleeping on as the earth turns.

For you, Buddhist. The awakened one,
Pain and its seasons in his opened eyes,
Looks out beyond the torpor of desire.

For me, tragic. While no claggy earth
Clings to his body, there's the weight and drag
Of the numb sleep he cannot wish to leave.

Or Christian. Death known, the tide of light
Revisits these abandoned earthly shores,
Infusing them, as ghostliness the flesh.

I dreamed we met in Borgo Sansepolcro
A second time, having again endured
The strange frustrations of the usual journey.

Such pleasure just to talk again! We strolled
In tears and laughter toward the city centre,
As if there'd been no breach. Just as before,

We stopped at an ordinary *trattoria* –
The meal we ate there far from commonplace –
Then on to the Palazzo Communale

For Piero's *Resurrection*. There it stood,
Just as recalled, a layer of tinted plaster
That opened up the surface of a wall

In the long council chamber, giving substance
And bulk to its alert protagonist.
The figures in the foreground were all sleeping

Like us, held there before them in a dream,
But where the last time we'd been struck with silence,
Each sunk within a vision, now we spoke.

First you to me (both looking at the picture):
'Where have you been these nine months?' And then I:
'I have been buried by the weight of darkness,

My wounds all stopped with earth. And what of you?'
'I slept and underwent the full gestation,
And now I wake, reborn from my own sleep.'

The risen Christ then vanished from the painting;
I woke alone and saw the empty frame,
For he and you had filled the world with absence.

XII
HEALER

A garden after nightfall rank with the smells
Of musk rose, honeysuckle and mock orange
Has eased its way into the front room

Of a terraced house the wrong side of the tracks.
From the kitchen you can hear an urgent sizzle,
Two boys are kicking a ball about in the yard

And a lone mother, wiping her busy hands,
Is taking on my pain. Intensely dark
And almost without highlights, her small eyes

Look into mine, their kindness inspires fear,
And talk of meridians and auric fields
Flutters weakly around their concentration –

Which is a concentration, you are sure,
That knows from the inside, works from the pain
That enters the world at birth. Therefore the hands

Held out above my wound radiate heat
And the room fills with a garden quite unknown
To the boys in the bare yard or the passers-by.

THE NAMES OF FLOWERS

Wild garlic, bugloss, toadflax – how you relished
The names of wayside flowers! It was as if,
In making words, your larynx, lips and tongue

A second time created the great world
And all its rich redundancy. We are
Sculptors of air and what we make is speech,

The given world as moulded to our needs
In our design. So coursing through our frames
The matter of our speech is briefly molten,

Soon to be set in grammar, prosody
And vocables. And so, in naming flowers,
Your beauty makes a beauty that knows theirs –

Teaches that what I name cannot be mine,
Who, living in my words as in the world,
Work to give utterance to that which is.

XIII
The Desert

You lead me to the desert. As we go,
You name the flowers we pass, gratuitous
In their abundance and variety.

But when the richness leaves us, you leave it,
And stone, sand, thorn and the stigmatic flesh
Become the matter of the universe.

Here is the proper place for meditation.
Where you confront the nothingness of things,
What space for someone added unto you?

*

And as for me, neither holy nor whole,
'My poetry is fragments, because I
Am fragments', yet the thought so often ours

Of being oned with God, your thought as mine,
Was brokenly revealed to me in all
The nothingness you brought upon my flesh.

Epilogue to 'Stigmata'

A blade
into your chest,
who drove it in?
An angel, I have said,
if there *are* angels.
Dante,
on the first
anniversary
of his grief,
drew an angel,
Beatrice
clear in his mind still.
Disturbed – 'Someone
was just with me,' he said –
he went on drawing, drawing
not yet writing.
You draw what you see,
but at times
not with the eye.
Dante, drawing,
knew her alive and,
knowing it,
wrote his poem.
Wounded,
writing it. For to see
without the eye
is to be pierced,
knife in the sternum.
Even so the angel
at La Verna
drove insight
into St Francis' side,
hands, feet.
So Pio. So Teresa.
Consummatum est
in the place of the skull.
You, walking with death,
know that place,

you who were there
in the cinema
looking away, sitting
that furnace of an afternoon
beside me but apart,
and it was then
I knew what I know.
Call it angel, call it love,
whatever:
the shaft
driven down into my body,
heart, bowels.
Too pure for me, you may be,
yet too wild – Eros
in each of us
diversely fierce –
too strong, too frail, too
holy not whole,
scourged by sorrow,
wounded by love –
but the shaft driven
into me, through me,
that tube of nothing,
fills with a long cry:
I, I love you, love you, love.
I, I love you, you.